A KID'S GUIDE TO FEELINGS

# FEELING MAD

BY KIRSTY HOLMES

KidHaven
PUBLISHING

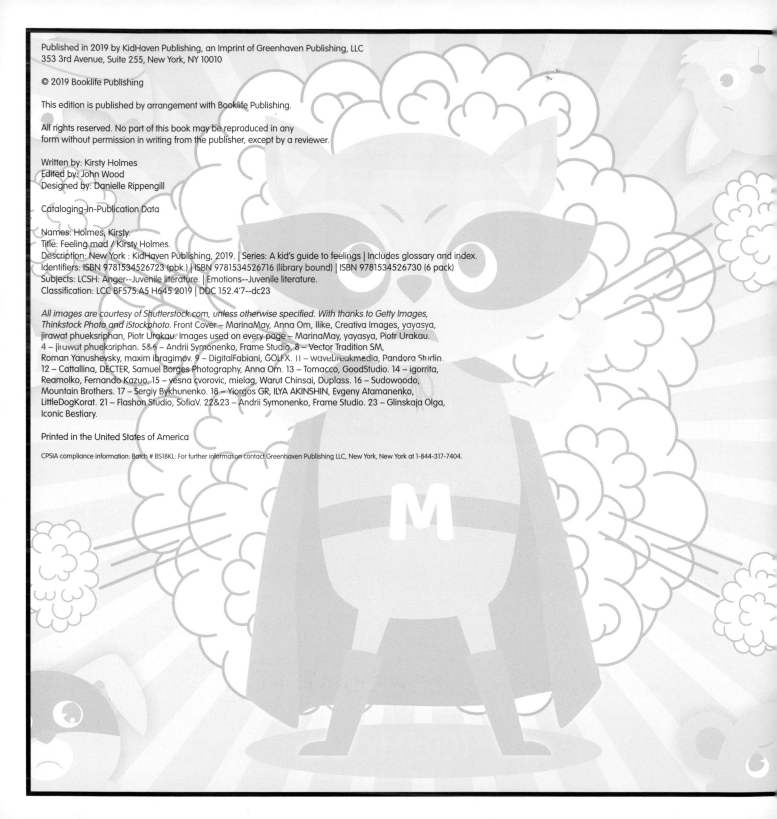

Published in 2019 by KidHaven Publishing, an Imprint of Greenhaven Publishing, LLC
353 3rd Avenue, Suite 255, New York, NY 10010

© 2019 Booklife Publishing

This edition is published by arrangement with Booklife Publishing.

Written by: Kirsty Holmes
Edited by: John Wood
Designed by: Danielle Rippengill

Cataloging-in-Publication Data

Names: Holmes, Kirsty.
Title: Feeling mad / Kirsty Holmes.
Description: New York : KidHaven Publishing, 2019. | Series: A kid's guide to feelings | Includes glossary and index.
Identifiers: ISBN 9781534526723 (pbk.) | ISBN 9781534526716 (library bound) | ISBN 9781534526730 (6 pack)
Subjects: LCSH: Anger--Juvenile literature. | Emotions--Juvenile literature.
Classification: LCC BF575.A5 H645 2019 | DDC 152.4'7--dc23

All images are courtesy of Shutterstock.com, unless otherwise specified. With thanks to Getty Images,
Thinkstock Photo and iStockphoto. Front Cover – MarinaMay, Anna Om, Ilike, Creativa Images, yayasya,
jirawat phueksriphan, Piotr Urakau. Images used on every page – MarinaMay, yayasya, Piotr Urakau.
4 – jirawat phueksriphan. 5&6 – Andrii Symonenko, Frame Studio. 8 – Vector Tradition SM,
Roman Yanushevsky, maxim ibragimov. 9 – DigitalFabiani, GOLFX. 11 – wavebreakmedia, Pandora Studio.
12 – Cattallina, DECTER, Samuel Borges Photography, Anna Om. 13 – Tomacco, GoodStudio. 14 – igorrita,
Reamolko, Fernando Kazuo. 15 – vesna cvorovic, mielag, Warut Chinsai, Duplass. 16 – Sudowoodo,
Mountain Brothers. 17 – Sergiy Bykhunenko. 18 – Yiorgos GR, ILYA AKINSHIN, Evgeny Atamanenko,
LittleDogKorat. 21 – Flashon Studio, SofiaV. 22&23 – Andrii Symonenko, Frame Studio. 23 – Glinskaja Olga,
Iconic Bestiary.

Printed in the United States of America

CPSIA compliance information: Batch # BS18KL: For further information contact Greenhaven Publishing LLC, New York, New York at 1-844-317-7404.

# CONTENTS

Words that look like **this** can be found in the glossary on page 24.

We all have **emotions**, or feelings, all the time. Our feelings are very important. They help us think about the world around us, and know how we want to **react**.

Sometimes, we feel good. Other times, we feel bad.

Everyone else is hiding from Raging Raccoon!
Our hero is feeling pretty mad!

Let's find out more... 7

# HOW DO WE FEEL WHEN WE'RE MAD?

Your heart beats really fast…

…you might feel **tense** or sick…

…you might want to shout…

… or you might want to hit, or throw things.

BAM!

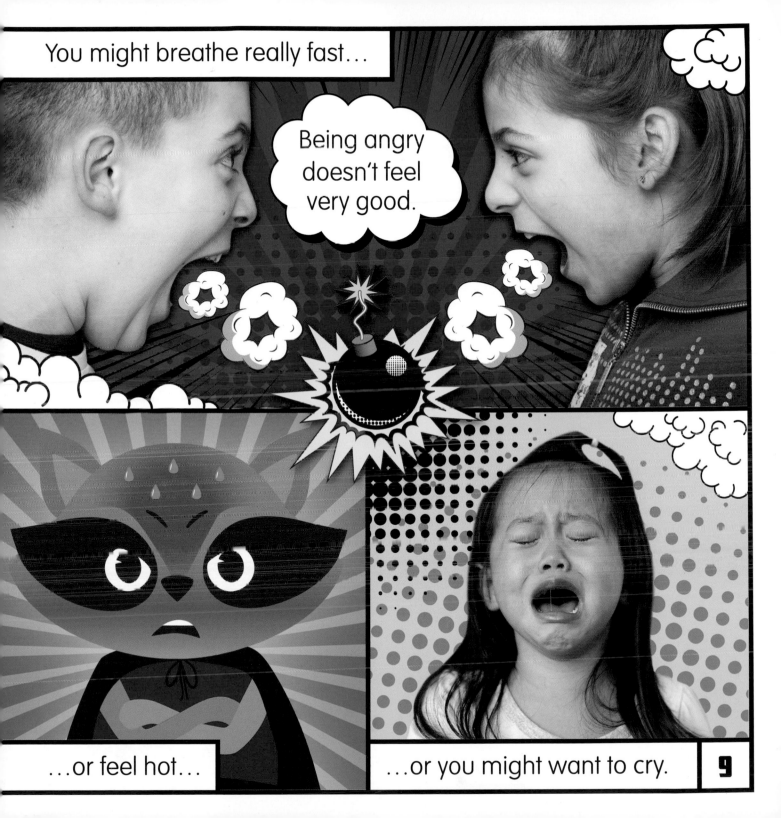

# HOW DO WE LOOK WHEN WE'RE MAD?

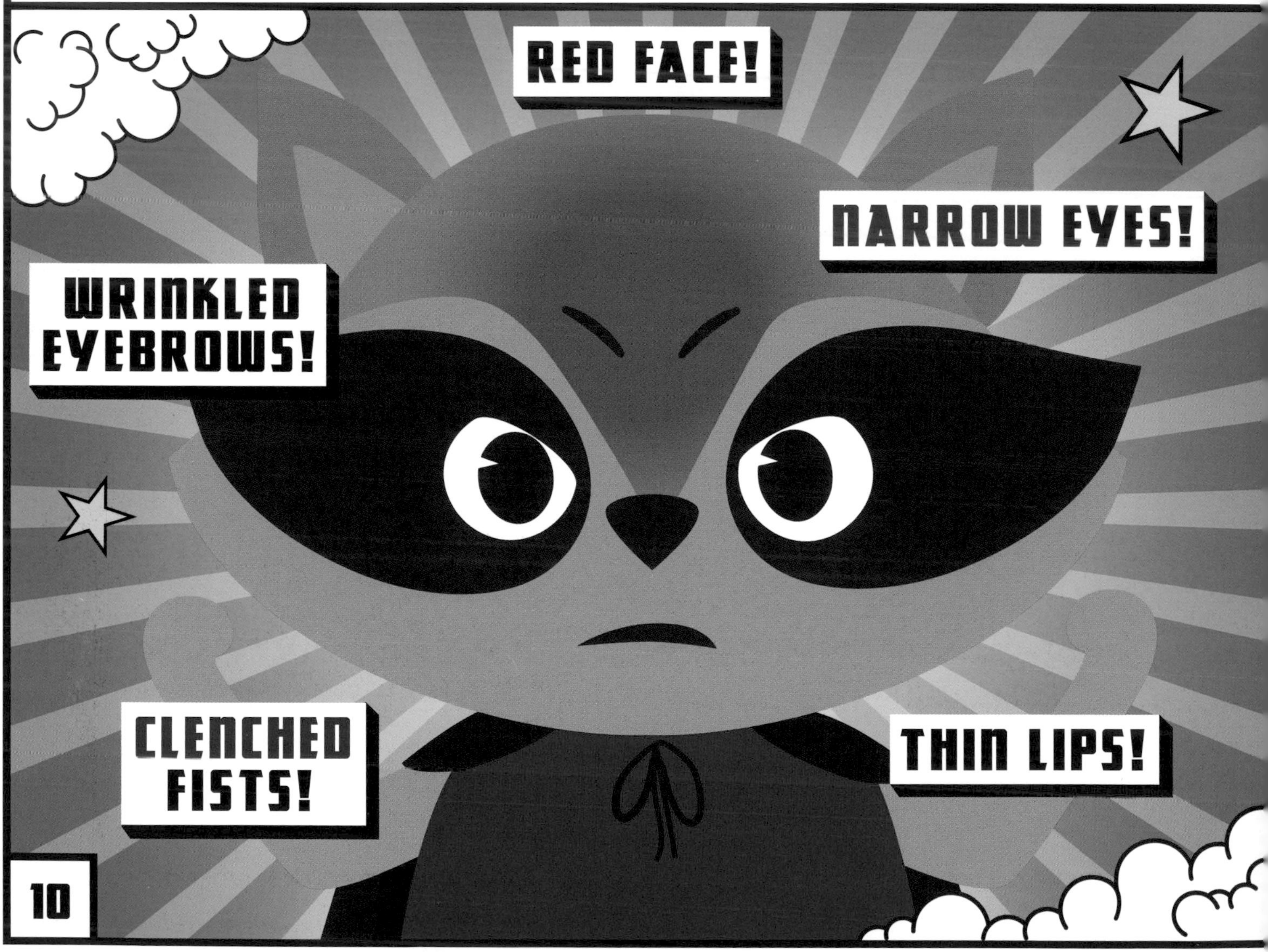

# WHY DO WE FEEL MAD?

**FEELING MAD IS AN IMPORTANT EMOTION.**

Thousands of years ago, humans lived in caves.

Lots of things were dangerous...

**GRRR!**

FIGHT SHOUT RUN ANGER

...so people **evolved** anger.

# THINGS THAT MAKE US MAD

# WHEN FEELING MAD IS GOOD

Feeling mad can be a good thing. If people feel mad about something, they might make sure it gets changed.

EQUAL CAKE
**FOR ALL**
RACCOONS!

Feeling mad can also help us to stand up for ourselves.

DON'T PUSH!

# WHEN FEELING MAD IS BAD

People get hurt.

Things get broken.

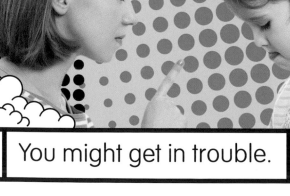

**18** You might get in trouble.

People can get upset.

You wouldn't want to play with someone who was angry all the time.

You shouldn't let your anger get out of control.

# DEALING WITH FEELINGS

# LET'S HELP!

Talking about your feelings can help you understand why you feel mad.

# GLOSSARY

| | |
|---|---|
| **BODY LANGUAGE** | things a person does with their body that tell you how they feel |
| **CLENCHED** | closed tightly shut |
| **EMOTIONS** | strong feelings such as joy, hate, sadness, or fear |
| **EVOLVED** | slowly developed over a long time |
| **FAIR** | being treated the same as others |
| **NARROW** | not wide; thin and small |
| **REACT** | to act or respond to something that has been done |
| **SURVIVE** | continue to live |
| **TENSE** | anxious or nervous |
| **THREATS** | things that can harm you |

# INDEX

24